COOL
jewels

BEADING
PROJECTS
FOR TEENS

NAOMI FUJIMOTO

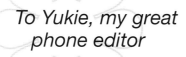

*To Yukie, my great
phone editor*

Printed in the United States of America.

11 10 09 08 07   1 2 3 4 5

Visit our Web site at kalmbachbooks.com. Secure online ordering available.

Publisher's Cataloging-In-Publication Data
(Prepared by The Donohue Group, Inc.)

Fujimoto, Naomi.
  Cool jewels : beading projects for teens / by Naomi Fujimoto.

  p. : ill. ; cm.

  Includes bibliographical references.
  ISBN: 978-0-87116-247-2

1. Beadwork. 2. Jewelry making. I. Title.

TT860 .F85 2007
745.58/2

Introduction

If you've ever admired a piece of jewelry and wondered how to create something like it for yourself, look no further. *Cool Jewels* will teach you how to make trendy jewelry with the hottest materials and very little effort.

Learn the skills you'll need and how to use them in fun, easy projects. I'll start with an explanation of supplies and techniques. Then, I'll walk you through making simple necklaces, bracelets, and earrings. Along the way, tips, bonus projects, and design ideas will help you get more out of your jewelry. Learn how to string a necklace, attach charms to a bracelet, and shape wire into clasps, bangles, and hoop earrings. The book also has great ideas for creating new jewels by recycling old jewelry or using vintage materials. No matter what your style is, you'll find lots of options for wearable jewelry.

I'll tell you where to shop for beads like mine, but these projects are really meant to be just a starting point for your own designs. Follow your instincts, and you'll have jewelry you love in a signature style. If your creativity needs a little help, you can find inspiration almost everywhere: in fabrics, paint swatches, nature, and even other jewelry. After you've tried a few projects, invite friends over for a beading party. Share your good ideas and good times.

I've been designing jewelry for years, and I have a few pieces I just can't live without. I wear them over and over. I hope this book encourages you to make something that becomes a favorite — your own cool jewels.

What's inside

GETTING STARTED

Walk into any bead or craft store, and you'll find lots of options for creating original jewelry. Crystals or gemstones, glass or metal – how do you know what to choose? Making jewelry is easy, but you should know a few basics before you get started. With just a few easy-to-find supplies and tools and some basic techniques, you can make any project in this book. In this chapter I'll show you:

- Basic bead types and shapes (p. 10)
- Different materials for stringing beads, charms, and pendants (p. 12)
- Basic tools for making jewelry (p. 13)
- Techniques for making the projects in this book (p. 14)

Start with beads

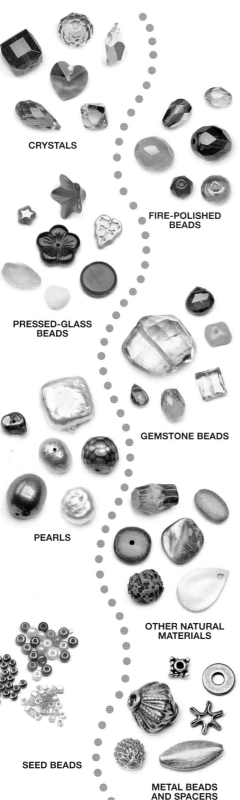

CRYSTALS

FIRE-POLISHED BEADS

PRESSED-GLASS BEADS

GEMSTONE BEADS

PEARLS

OTHER NATURAL MATERIALS

SEED BEADS

METAL BEADS AND SPACERS

You can find beads made from just about any material, in any size, color, or shape. In addition to the familiar round and oval bead shapes, some others you might want to try are: briolette (top-drilled faceted teardrop), chip, nugget, rondelle, and rectangle. There are so many beads, I don't have room to show all of them, but here are a few.

crystals

A crystal is a faceted glass bead with a high lead content. The lead is what makes crystals sparkle. Crystals are available in a wide range of colors and shapes and with different finishes. AB (aurora borealis), for example, has a rainbow-like shine. Swarovski, the largest crystal manufacturer, cuts its crystals by machine. This means the crystals are uniform in shape and color — handy if you're looking for the same bead a few months later. Look for bicone crystals (pointy on each end), rounds, cubes, and other shapes for your jewelry.

fire-polished beads

Fire-polished beads are similar to crystals, but they don't have the high lead content. Instead, these glass beads are tumbled in a heated container (kind of like laundry in a dryer) to make them sparkle, so their facets have softer edges. Fire-polished beads are available in a variety of sizes, shapes, and finishes.

pressed-glass beads

Pressed-glass beads are created in molds, so they come in a range of fun and creative shapes. Look for flowers, leaves, hearts, stars, and more in both translucent and opaque glass. Keep an eye out for vintage glass beads, too; some of them were made in molds that aren't around anymore.

gemstone beads

Gemstones offer plenty of colors and shapes. These beads can be polished, unpolished, faceted, or smooth, so you're sure to find the right texture for the look you want. Gemstones are often sold in strands. A 16-in. (41cm) strand is pretty standard, but briolettes and other pricier beads are usually sold in shorter strands with plastic or metal spacers between beads. Many gemstones are treated to brighten their color or to make them more durable.

pearls

Natural and dyed pearls come in a wide range of colors and styles. While the most familiar shapes are round, potato (oval), and button (flattened rounds), you also can find shapes like coins or teardrops and even faceted pearls. If you need perfectly round pearls (say, for a multistrand necklace), buy man-made glass pearls or shell pearls.

other natural materials

If you like a natural look, try beads carved from organic materials like bone, horn, nut, seed, shell, or wood. Since they were made by nature, beads on a strand will probably differ a little in size and shape. Buy enough for your project the first time, since it can be hard to return to the store and get a perfect match.

seed beads

Seed beads are tiny glass beads that are made in a range of sizes, from 6º to 15º. Seed bead sizes are measured with aught symbols (º); the bigger the number, the smaller the bead (an 8º seed bead is larger than an 11º). They are sold by the hank (a group of strands) or by gram weight and come in an amazing range of colors and finishes. Most seed beads come from the Czech Republic or Japan. Japanese seed beads are very consistent in size, so use them when uniformity is important (like when you need several strands to match). Try seed beads as spacers between larger beads.

metal beads and spacers

Beads and spacers can be made of base metal, silver, or gold. Base metal beads include steel, copper, brass, tin, and nickel. Although base metals are less expensive, they don't wear as well as precious metal. Silver beads are usually .925 sterling, meaning they are 92.5% silver. The silver is alloyed (mixed) with another metal, which makes it stronger. Handmade Bali-silver beads often have a darker color than sterling silver because they are oxidized. Hill Tribe silver is usually purer than .925 sterling. If you like gold, try vermeil (pronounced "ver-may"), which is a coating of gold over sterling silver. You can also try silver- or gold-plated beads, which are cheaper than sterling silver or gold-filled. Unless you're making mixed-metal jewelry, try to match the metal beads with the crimp beads and clasp.

Add some findings

"Findings" is a general term for jewelry pieces like clasps and head pins, but people sometimes use the word differently. So if you're looking for something specific, look for the product by name; it may or may not be considered a finding.

head pins and eye pins

A head pin is a wire with a little nub at one end. It looks like a long, skinny nail. You'll need head pins to string beads for dangles. Although they come in different gauges and lengths, you can use 1½–2-in. (3.8–5cm) 22- or 24-gauge head pins for most projects (see p. 12 to learn about wire gauges).

The eye pin is the head pin's cousin. Instead of a nub at the end, there's a loop. If you need to make lots of links, using eye pins may save you time, but I don't think they're a must-have. You can make eye pins with wire by making a plain loop (see Basics, p. 14) at one end.

jump rings

Jump rings are small wire rings that you use to link things together (like connecting a clasp to the end of a chain). They come in different shapes, but you'll use round and oval jump rings the most. Oval jump rings are good for projects that may have a lot of stress on them, like charms on a bracelet. (If your bracelet gets caught on your sleeve, an oval jump ring will have a better hold than a round one because the charm won't pull at the join where the ends of the ring meet.) You can use 3–4mm jump rings to attach a lightweight chain to a clasp; 6–7mm jump rings work better for heavier projects.

soldered jump rings

A soldered jump ring is a jump ring that's permanently closed. Use one opposite a lobster claw clasp when you finish a necklace or a bracelet (it's much more secure than a regular jump ring). You also can hammer soldered jump rings and use them as part of your design.

crimp beads

You'll need crimp beads to finish projects strung on flexible beading wire. Crimp beads are small, thin-walled metal tubes that grip the wire and hold it in place when flattened or folded with pliers. If you use round crimp beads, flatten them with chainnose pliers. If you use crimp tubes, you can use chainnose pliers or crimping pliers. Crimping pliers make a folded crimp, which looks professional and can also be hidden inside a large-hole bead. (See Basics, p. 14, for more on crimping.)

crimp ends

Crimp ends give a pretty finish to leather or suede. They are metal coils or tubes that you put the cord into, then flatten. Each crimp end has a loop for attaching a clasp. You can also use folded crimp ends, which fold around the cord. Larger crimp ends can handle multiple cords.

pinch end caps

Pinch end caps are like crimp ends. You use them with ribbons or thick cords. Use your chainnose pliers to close them; they have teeth that grab the ribbon.

earring findings

I use "earring wire" to refer to hook-style wires, sometimes called "French ear wires," which are great for making dangling earrings. You can use other kinds of earring findings for these projects. Try earring posts; they have ear nuts that go on the back. Lever-back earring wires, with a hinged opening, are also an option. Earring threads are popular; they have a chain that goes through your ear.

clasps

You'll need a clasp to connect the ends of your necklace or bracelet. For a simple, secure hold, I like lobster claw clasps. Clasps aren't just something to be hidden at the back of a necklace, though. There are pretty toggle clasps, magnetic clasps, slide clasps, box clasps, and hook-and-eye clasps with details like wirework or beads. Sometimes a pretty clasp can be worn in the front, changing the look of your piece.

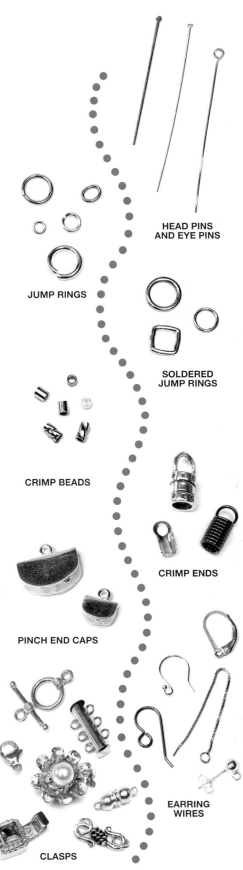

HEAD PINS AND EYE PINS

JUMP RINGS

SOLDERED JUMP RINGS

CRIMP BEADS

CRIMP ENDS

PINCH END CAPS

EARRING WIRES

CLASPS

String everything on

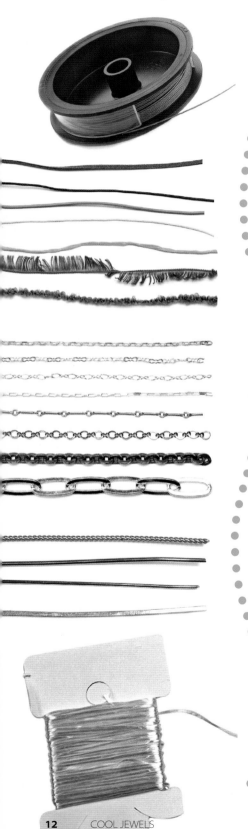

You can string beads on many different materials, and manufacturers are always developing new products you can use to make jewelry. Here are the most common stringing materials.

flexible beading wire

Flexible beading wire is made of wires twisted together and coated with nylon. It's stronger than thread and doesn't stretch. The higher the strand count (three to 49 strands), the more flexible and kink-resistant the wire. The wire's diameter is measured in inches (for example, .012 means that the wire has a diameter of .012 inches). Use .012 to string lightweight beads or beads with small holes (like pearls). For most projects, I use Soft Flex or Beadalon .014 or .015, but I'll use .018, .019, or .024 for heavier beads. For projects where the wire is visible, try gold- or silver-coated varieties. You don't need a needle when you're stringing with beading wire; just pick up the beads with the end of the wire.

leather, suede, and fibers

Leather and suede offer colorful options for earthy-looking jewelry. Waxed cotton and linen cords are stronger than leather or suede, so they also are good choices. Ribbons and yarns come in many colors and styles, from super skinny to extra wide. You can either tie the ends of the fiber together and go, or attach a crimp end or pinch end cap for a professional-looking, longer-lasting finish.

chain

Chain is available in many styles and finishes, including sterling silver and gold-filled as well as base metal or plated styles. (I love how chain darkens with age. I'm always on the lookout for vintage chain.) The most basic style is cable chain, but there are many other options out there. You can buy chain by the foot and attach your own clasp.

wire

Wire comes in a range of hardnesses, including dead-soft, half-hard, and full-hard. The softer the wire, the easier it is to shape. Half-hard wire is still easy to shape, but it can withstand some stress, so it works well for most projects. Wire hardens as you work with it. Hardening strengthens the wire, but too much hardening makes the wire brittle and breakable (keep that in mind if you hammer it). Wire is available in different gauges: the higher the number, the finer the wire. I like to keep a few feet of sterling silver and gold-filled around in 22- and 24-gauges – perfect for creating loops and dangles. You can find wire in many different shapes, too. Round is the most common, but half-round, square, triangular, and twisted wires make for fun design options. Practice working with inexpensive craft or copper wire before you try more expensive silver or gold varieties.

ribbon elastic

Use ribbon elastic to make stretch bracelets; you won't need a clasp. Ribbon elastic works best with beads that have smooth holes; jagged holes can nick the elastic and make it break. You should string on a doubled strand for added strength. Make sure to knot the ends and apply glue to the knot. If you're using beads with large holes, you can hide the knot inside one of the beads.

Use these tools

Beading tools make it easy to shape wire, open and close jump rings, and put your pieces together. What's absolutely necessary? Chainnose pliers, roundnose pliers, and diagonal wire cutters. That's all you need to get started.

chainnose pliers

These pliers have smooth, flat inside jaws and a narrow tip. You'll need them to make loops and to open and close jump rings. You can also flatten crimp beads with them.

roundnose pliers

Roundnose pliers have round jaws; you'll use them to make loops. The size of the loops depends on what part of the jaws you use. You may want to spend a little more money to buy a good pair (I like Lindstrom pliers). Look for pliers that have precise, round jaws that taper to a sharp point – great for making consistent round loops.

diagonal wire cutters

The angled blades on diagonal wire cutters let you trim wire very close. Flexible beading wire will dull lightweight cutters, so think about getting a heavier pair.

While you can make everything in this book with the tools I just mentioned, here are a few extra ones that are nice to have as well.

crimping pliers

Crimping pliers have jaws with two notches so you can make folded crimps. If you don't want to get a pair just yet, you can make flattened crimps with your chainnose pliers.

calipers

Calipers are a bead-measuring tool. You put the bead in the jaws, then read the number to figure out its size. Since I order a lot of stuff online and beads aren't usually shown at their actual size, calipers help me picture the bead sizes before I buy.

glue

Glue helps keep knots closed. G-S Hypo Cement comes in a tube with a tiny tip, so it's easy to apply just a drop.

twisted-wire beading needles

These are flexible needles that are handy for stringing beads on ribbon elastic. They have a large eye that is easy to thread, and it collapses to go through small bead holes.

hammer

You'll need a hammer with a flat head to harden wire for hoops and bangles. The hammer shown here is a ball-peen hammer, which you can find at the hardware store. It's nice and light, which makes it great for jewelry making. Make sure the head of your hammer is free of nicks (household hammers often have marks from use, and these can mar your metal).

bench block or anvil

A bench block gives you a flat, solid surface (usually steel) to hammer wire on. You can also use an anvil, which you can shape wire or metal around — but a bench block is cheaper and is all you'll need for these projects.

metal file

When you're working with wire, you may need to file rough edges, like the ends of homemade earring wires. If you do a lot of wirework, you can buy jeweler's files, like those shown here. For the projects in this book, an emery board (nail file) will do just fine.

scissors

Get a sharp pair of scissors for cutting fibers, leather, and threads (Fiskars are good). Dull scissors will drive you crazy when you try to cut ribbon.

bead design board

Design boards have grooves in them for strands of beads, which is convenient when you're making a multistrand necklace. It will help you see what the necklace will look like when worn. A design board isn't necessary, but it's handy. You can also use a towel or a piece of felt to lay out your designs.

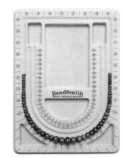

Basics

You only need to learn a few techniques to make your own jewelry. These techniques are pretty easy, but don't worry if you need to practice to get them right – a little practice will ensure that your jewelry looks great and lasts a long time. As I use these techniques in projects, I'll remind you to come back to this section if you need help.

cutting flexible beading wire

Decide how long you want your finished necklace or bracelet to be. Add 6 in. (15cm) for a necklace or 5 in. (13cm) for a bracelet. Use diagonal wire cutters to cut a piece of beading wire to that length. (For example, for a 15-in./38cm necklace, cut 21 in./53cm of beading wire.)

checking the fit

Tape the ends of the strand. Put the strand around your neck or your wrist and see how it looks. Leave about 1 in. (2.5cm) for the clasp. If you need to, add or remove beads from each end.

overhand knot

Make a loop and pass the working end through it. Pull the ends to tighten the knot.

surgeon's knot

Cross the right end over the left and go through the loop. Go through again. Pull the ends to tighten the knot. Cross the left end over the right and go through. Tighten the knot.

flattened crimp

Before crimping, tighten the beading wire to form a small loop. Make sure that the wire is flexible: don't overtighten it, but don't leave big gaps.

1 Hold the crimp bead with the tip of your chainnose pliers. Squeeze the pliers firmly to flatten the crimp bead, being careful not to squeeze the surrounding beads.

2 Tug the beading wire to make sure the crimp has a solid grip. If the wire slides, remove the crimp bead and repeat the steps with a new crimp bead.

folded crimp

1 Position the crimp bead in the notch closest to the crimping pliers' handle.

2 Separate the wires and firmly squeeze the crimp bead.

3 Move the crimp bead into the notch at the pliers' tip, holding the crimp bead. Squeeze the pliers, folding the bead in half.

4 Tug the beading wire to make sure the crimp has a solid grip. If the wire slides, remove the crimp bead and repeat the steps with a new crimp bead. (For extra security, squeeze the folded crimp with chainnose pliers.)

opening & closing jump rings

1 Hold the jump ring with two pairs of chainnose pliers or with chainnose and roundnose pliers.

2 To open the jump ring, bring one pair of pliers toward you and push the other pair away. (Don't try to unroll the jump ring. It won't come back to its original shape.) Reverse the steps to close the jump ring.

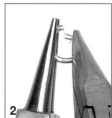

plain loop

1 Trim the wire ⅜ in. (1cm) above the top bead. Make a right-angle bend close to the bead.
2 Grab the wire's tip with roundnose pliers. Roll the wire around the jaw to form a half circle.
3 Release the wire. Move the pliers to grip the center of the loop, and continue rolling.
4 The finished loop should be a centered circle above the bead.

1

2

3

4

wrapped loop

1 Make sure there's at least 1¼ in. (3.2cm) of wire above the bead. With the tip of your chainnose pliers, grab the wire directly above the bead. Bend the wire against the pliers into a right angle.
2 Position the roundnose pliers in the bend as shown.
3 Pull the wire over the top jaw of the pliers.
4 Reposition the pliers so that the lower jaw is in the curve. Wrap the wire snugly around the lower jaw of the pliers. You have just made the first half of a wrapped loop. It should be centered over the bead. (If you need to connect the loop to a chain or other component, do it now.)

5 To complete the wrapped loop, hold the loop with chainnose pliers, as shown. Using your roundnose pliers, wrap the wire tail around the wire stem, covering the stem between the loop and the bead. The wraps should be tight and close together.
6 Trim the extra wrapping wire, and press the end close to the stem with chainnose pliers.

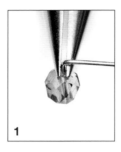

1

2

3

4

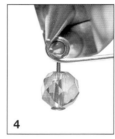

5

6

wraps above a top-drilled bead

1 Center a top-drilled bead on a 3-in. (7.6cm) piece of wire. Bend each wire upward around the bead, crossing the wires into an X.
2 Using chainnose pliers, make a small bend in each wire so the ends form a right angle.
3 Wrap the horizontal wire around the vertical wire like in a wrapped loop. Trim the extra wrapping wire. Press the end close to the stem with chainnose pliers.

1

2

3

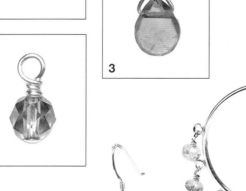

NECKLACES

Whether you like your necklaces short, long, or somewhere in between, wearing one creates immediate impact. In this chapter, I'll show you how to string necklaces on chain, leather, ribbon, and flexible beading wire. Don't forget, you can change the beads or the length of the necklace in any of these designs to fit your own style – so you'll have plenty of jewelry for school and special occasions. Here are some of the things you'll learn to do:

- Attach tokens and crystals to a chain (p. 20)
- Tie a pendant on leather (p. 22)
- String oversized metallic pearls (p. 24)
- Knot chunky wood beads on ribbon (p. 32)
- Make your own clasp for a necklace (p. 40)

Round and round

Round beads are great to work with. You can find them in different materials, textures, and colors — and in the same sizes. For a fun necklace, combine gumball-sized gemstone, rattan, and crochet beads. A glass disk pendant plays up the shapes and colors of the beads.

tip *When you're tightening the wires, make sure the necklace is in a curved position (like it will be when you wear it). Otherwise, the wire will be too tight.*

1 Cut a 4-in. (10cm) piece of 22-gauge wire. String a pendant and make a set of wraps above it (see Basics, p. 14).

2 Make a wrapped loop (Basics) above the wraps, perpendicular to the pendant.

3 Decide how long you want your necklace to be, add 6 in. (15cm), and cut a piece of beading wire to that length. (My necklace is 15½ in./ 39.4cm.) Center the pendant and a seed bead on the wire.

4 On one end, string a gemstone bead, a crochet bead, two gemstones, and a rattan bead. On the other end, string two gemstones, a rattan bead, a gemstone, and a crochet bead. Repeat until the strand is within 1 in. (2.5cm) of the length you want your necklace to be.

5 On one end, string a spacer, a crimp bead, a spacer, and a lobster claw clasp. Repeat on the other end, using a 2–3-in. (5–7.6cm) piece of chain in place of the clasp. Check the fit (Basics). Go back through the beads just strung and tighten the wire. Crimp the crimp beads (Basics) and trim the extra wire.

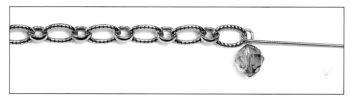

6 On a head pin, string an accent bead. Make the first half of a wrapped loop. Attach the dangle to the chain and complete the wraps.

supplies

- 35–40mm disk-shaped pendant (all beads from Planet Bead)
- 16-in. (41cm) strand 16mm round gemstone beads
- **8–10** 16mm round beads, in two materials (such as rattan and crochet)
- 6–8mm accent bead
- 11° seed bead
- 4 3–4mm spacers
- flexible beading wire, .018 or .019
- 4 in. (10cm) 22-gauge half-hard wire
- 1½-in. (3.8cm) head pin
- 2 crimp beads
- lobster claw clasp
- 2–3 in. (5–7.6cm) chain, 5–6mm links
- chainnose pliers
- roundnose pliers
- diagonal wire cutters
- crimping pliers (optional)

another project Make a bracelet with leftover beads. It can be hard to adjust the length of bracelets made with large beads – adding or subtracting one bead makes a big difference. To make sizing your bracelet easier, use a chain extender.

Show your love with chain trinkets

Tokens of your affection

A subway token, a zodiac pendant, or a charm dangle tells a story about you. Wear a personal trinket close to your heart. (I love my subway-token necklace – I wear it almost every day.) Make a bunch of necklaces. Some days, a single charm will say enough. Other days, you'll want to layer them. Anything you can attach with a jump ring can be converted into wearable jewelry.

tip *Use a chain that's strong yet delicate. I like cable chain with 2–4mm links. To lend a well-loved look to your necklace, use vintage chain, which you can find at thrift stores.*

1 **token necklace** Open a 6–7mm jump ring (see Basics, p. 14). Attach a token and close the jump ring. Decide how long you want your necklace to be, and cut a piece of chain to that length. (The key necklace is 17 in./43cm; the subway-token necklace, 18 in./46cm.)

2 Center the token on the chain. Use a 6–7mm jump ring to attach a second token to a link of chain about 1 in. (2.5cm) from the center.

3 Check the fit, allowing ½ in. (1.3cm) for the clasp. Trim chain from both sides, if you need to. Use a 3–4mm jump ring to attach a lobster claw clasp to one end. Repeat on the other end, using a soldered jump ring in place of the clasp.

1 **zodiac necklace** On a head pin, string a crystal. Make a wrapped loop (Basics) big enough to slide over the chain. Repeat with a second crystal.

2 Open a 6–7mm jump ring (Basics). Attach a zodiac pendant and close the jump ring. Decide how long you want your necklace to be, and cut a piece of chain to that length. (My necklace is 16 in./41cm.) Center a crystal unit, the pendant, and a crystal unit on the chain. Finish as in step 3 of the token necklace.

supplies

token necklace
- 2 subway tokens or other charms
- 15–18 in. (38–46cm) chain, 3–4mm links
- 2 6–7mm oval jump rings
- 2 3–4mm jump rings
- lobster claw clasp and soldered jump ring
- chainnose pliers
- roundnose pliers
- diagonal wire cutters

zodiac necklace
- 18mm zodiac pendant (Artbeads.com)
- 2 4–6mm crystals
- 15–18 in. (38–46cm) chain, 2–3mm links
- 2 1½-in. (3.8cm) head pins
- 6–7mm oval jump ring
- 2 3–4mm jump rings
- lobster claw clasp and soldered jump ring
- chainnose pliers
- roundnose pliers
- diagonal wire cutters

design idea
Try pairing birthstones with a zodiac pendant for a personalized necklace. Here are the traditional birthstones for each month. You can also use beads in the same colors.

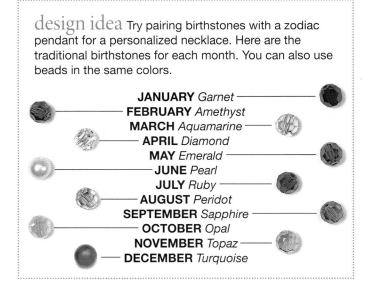

JANUARY *Garnet*
FEBRUARY *Amethyst*
MARCH *Aquamarine*
APRIL *Diamond*
MAY *Emerald*
JUNE *Pearl*
JULY *Ruby*
AUGUST *Peridot*
SEPTEMBER *Sapphire*
OCTOBER *Opal*
NOVEMBER *Topaz*
DECEMBER *Turquoise*

Tie up a quick necklace

Knot this time

Make a casual necklace in just a few minutes. All you need to do is knot a pendant on some leather cord. Leather comes in many shades, so you can match your pendant and cord or use a contrasting color for more drama. Finish with crimp ends and a clasp for a professional touch.

supplies

- 35–50mm pendant with a 7mm or larger hole at the top (round shell pendant, Fire Mountain Gems; carved drop pendant, Beadissimo)
- 16–20 in. (41–51cm) leather cord, 1–2mm (Land of Odds)
- **2** 3–4mm jump rings
- **2** crimp ends (Rio Grande)
- lobster claw clasp and soldered jump ring
- chainnose pliers
- roundnose pliers
- G-S Hypo Cement

1 Decide how long you want your necklace to be, add 1 in. (2.5cm), and cut a piece of leather cord to that length. (My necklaces are 16 in./41cm.) Fold the cord in half. String both ends through a pendant. Pull the cord ends through the fold, and gently tighten the knot.

2 Check the fit. The clasp will add about 1 in. (2.5cm) to the finished length. Trim the cord if you need to. On each end, apply glue. Attach a crimp end, and flatten the center (crimp portion) with chainnose pliers.

tips *If the pendant is heavy, use waxed cotton or linen cord instead of leather — both are stronger.*

Try bookend-style crimp ends. Use your chainnose pliers to fold down each side of the crimp end around the leather; squeeze firmly.

design idea

To dress up the look, try chain instead of leather. Use cable chain with 3–4mm links for a knot that hugs the pendant nicely.

3 Open a 3–4mm jump ring (see Basics, p. 14). Attach a lobster claw clasp to one end of the necklace and close the jump ring. Repeat on the other end, using a soldered jump ring in place of the clasp.

String an oversized-pearl necklace

Pearls for girls

A necklace with big, multicolored pearls is a fun answer to Mom's classic strand. This is a really quick, super-easy necklace to make — you'll just string pearls and crystals. It may become an everyday favorite, but it's especially flattering on picture day or for a special occasion.

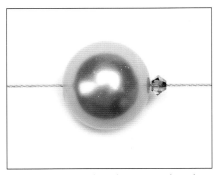

1 Decide how long you want your necklace to be, add 6 in. (15cm), and cut a piece of beading wire to that length (see Basics, p. 14). (My necklace is 16½ in./42cm.) Center a bicone crystal, a pearl, and a bicone on the wire.

2 On each end, string a pearl and a bicone. Repeat until the strand is within 1 in. (2.5cm) of the length you want your necklace to be. End with a pearl.

3 Check the fit (Basics). On each end, string a spacer, a crimp bead, a spacer, and half of the clasp. Go back through the beads just strung and tighten the wire. Crimp the crimp bead (Basics) and trim the extra wire.

tip *To make sure the design stays balanced, use a toggle clasp with a loop that's about the same size as one of the pearls.*

another project You can make earrings out of leftover pearls. Simply string a pearl and a crystal on a decorative head pin, make a wrapped loop above the beads, and attach the dangle to an earring wire.

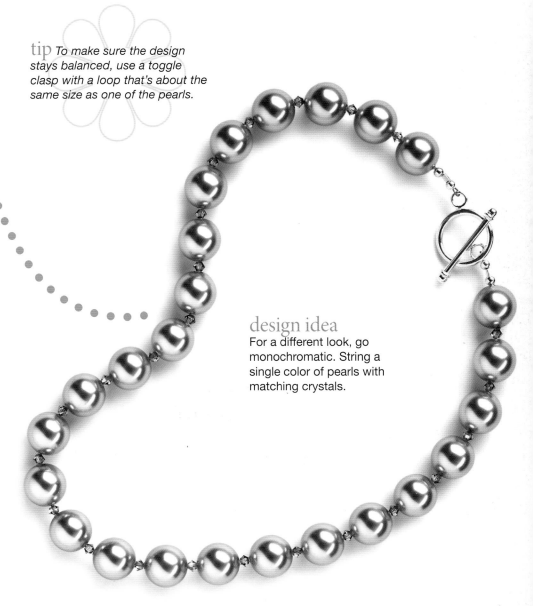

design idea
For a different look, go monochromatic. String a single color of pearls with matching crystals.

supplies

- 16-in. (41cm) strand 10–14mm round shell pearls (Soft Flex)
- **22–30** 3mm bicone crystals
- **4** 4mm spacers
- flexible beading wire, .018 or .019
- **2** crimp beads
- toggle clasp
- chainnose pliers or crimping pliers
- diagonal wire cutters

Crystals float on a chain necklace

tip *To keep the necklace lightweight, use only a few beads. Otherwise, the beaded part may pull the chain too tightly around your neck.*

Lightweight lariat

A lariat is a long necklace without a clasp that you can wrap and tie in different ways (picture a lasso). This necklace has the look of a lariat without all the wrapping and knotting. You won't need a clasp. Instead, one end slips through a hammered jump ring to display a smattering of tiny beads. Just make sure to skip a link or two between beads so that each one can fit through the jump ring.

1 On a head pin, string a bead. Make the first half of a wrapped loop (see Basics, p. 14). Make three to five more dangles.

2 Decide how long you want your lariat to be and cut a piece of chain to that length. (My lariat is 18 in./46cm.) Open a 3–4mm jump ring (Basics). Attach a briolette to one end of the chain, and close the jump ring.

3 One or two links away from the briolette, attach a dangle. Complete the wraps.

4 Attach the rest of the dangles. (I like to put the bigger beads closer to the bottom of the lariat.)

5 On a bench block or anvil, hammer a 9–12mm jump ring. Flip the jump ring over and hammer the other side.

6 Check the fit, and trim chain if you need to. Use a 3–4mm jump ring to attach the end of the chain to the hammered jump ring.

supplies

- 5.5 x 11mm crystal briolette (Fusion Beads)
- **4–6** 4–8mm beads (sizes can vary, but each has to fit through the hammered jump ring)
- 18–27 in. (46–69cm) chain, 3–5mm links (crinkle chain from House of Gems)
- **4–6** 1½-in. (3.8cm) head pins
- 9–12mm soldered jump ring (Rio Grande)
- **2** 3–4mm jump rings
- chainnose pliers
- roundnose pliers
- diagonal wire cutters
- hammer
- bench block or anvil

design idea For a clean, modern design, attach only one bead to the chain. (I attached a 13mm Swarovski polygon drop bead to a 22-in./56cm piece of chain.) You can also try a cubic zirconia drop (available from Lima Beads).

Silk ribbon shows off a handmade bead centerpiece

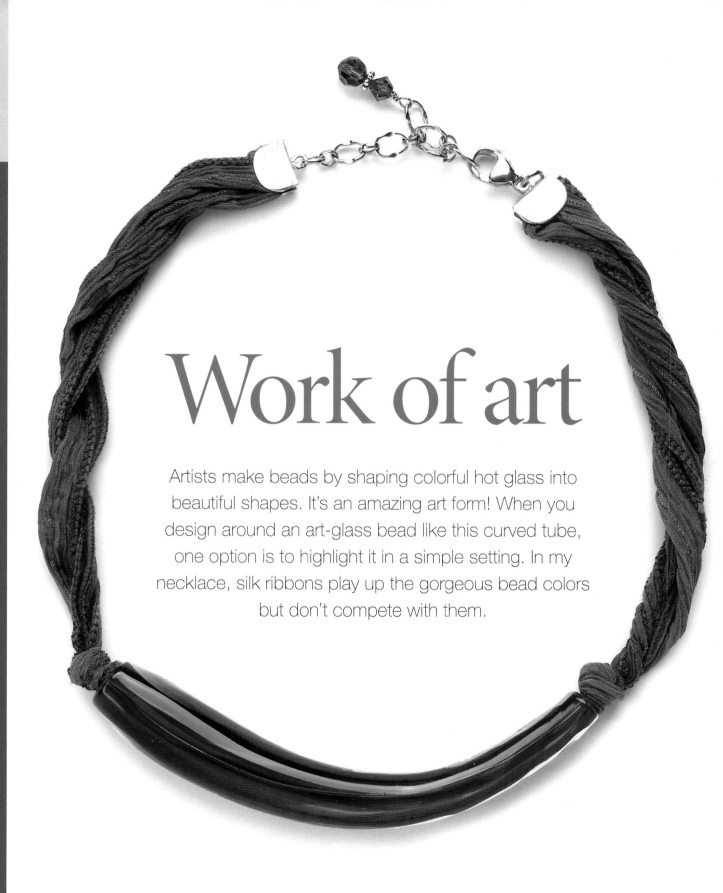

Work of art

Artists make beads by shaping colorful hot glass into beautiful shapes. It's an amazing art form! When you design around an art-glass bead like this curved tube, one option is to highlight it in a simple setting. In my necklace, silk ribbons play up the gorgeous bead colors but don't compete with them.

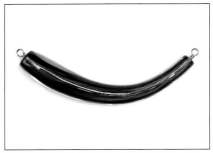

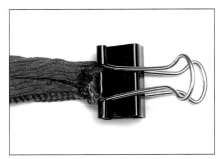

1 Cut an 8-in. (20cm) piece of wire. Make a 4–5mm wrapped loop (see Basics, p. 14) on one end. Curve the wire slightly and gently string a tube-shaped bead. Make a 4–5mm wrapped loop on the other end.

2 Cut a 1-yd. (.9m) ribbon in half. Center one of the wire loops on a ribbon. With both ends, tie an overhand knot (Basics). As you tighten the knot, cover the wire loop. Attach the second ribbon with an overhand knot.

3 Check the fit, and trim the ribbon ends to the length of your necklace. (My necklace is 14¼ in./36.2cm plus the extender.) Apply glue to the ribbon ends and fold each pair together three or four times. Clip a binder clip over the fold and allow the glue to dry.

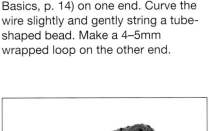

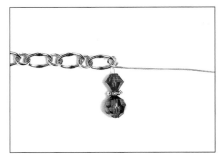

4 Remove the binder clips. On each end, attach a pinch end cap. Close the end cap with chainnose pliers.

5 On one end, open a jump ring (Basics) and attach a lobster claw clasp. Close the jump ring. Repeat on the other end, using a 2–3-in. (5–7.6cm) chain in place of the clasp.

6 On a head pin, string accent beads and spacers. Make the first half of a wrapped loop. Attach the dangle to the chain and complete the wraps.

supplies

- curved glass tube-shaped bead, approximately 100mm long (Olive Glass)
- **3** 4–8mm accent beads and spacers
- 1-yd. (.9m) ribbon, ⅝ in. (1.6cm) wide (Da Beads)
- 8 in. (20cm) 20- or 22-gauge half-hard wire
- 2-in. (5cm) head pin
- **2** 3–4mm jump rings
- **2** 11mm pinch end caps (Rio Grande)
- lobster claw clasp
- 2–3-in. (5–7.6cm) chain, 5–6mm links
- chainnose pliers
- roundnose pliers
- diagonal wire cutters
- scissors
- Barge cement
- binder clips

tip *You can string ribbons through the bead instead of through wire loops. For easier stringing, tape the ribbon ends and cut a point.*

design idea You can highlight different colors and textures by including wool, cotton, or metallic yarns with the ribbons. Shop Earth Echoes for a selection of ribbons and yarns.

Lucite brights

Not only is Lucite vibrant, but its seamless surface looks flawless (unlike other plastics). To make an eye-catching necklace, use bright-colored rings in a single shade or use multiple hues. These cheery rings perk up a vintage chain and give the necklace a retro feel.

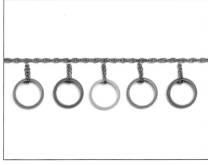

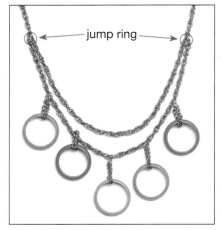

1 Cut an 8-in. (20cm) piece of 4–5mm chain and a 14–17 in. (36–43cm) piece. Cut five 1-in. (2.5cm) pieces of 3–4mm chain. On a short chain, string a Lucite ring. Open a jump ring (see Basics, p. 14). Attach the ends of the short chain to the center of the 8-in. (20cm) chain. Close the jump ring.

2 On each side of the first ring, use jump rings to attach Lucite rings with short chains, about 1 in. (2.5cm) apart.

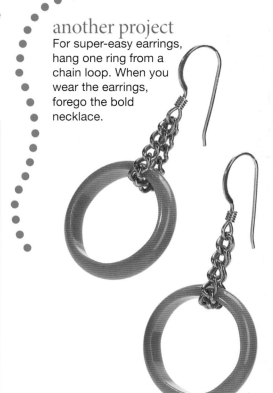

3 Decide how long you want your necklace to be, and cut the 14–17 in. (36–43cm) chain to that length. (My necklace is 14 in./36cm.) Use a jump ring to attach each end of the 8-in. (20cm) chain to the necklace chain. Check the fit, and trim chain from each end if you need to.

4 On one end, use a jump ring to attach a lobster claw clasp.

5 On the other end, use a jump ring to attach a 2–3-in. (5–7.6cm) piece of 5–6mm chain. On a head pin, string an accent bead. Make the first half of a wrapped loop (Basics). Attach the dangle to the chain and complete the wraps.

another project

For super-easy earrings, hang one ring from a chain loop. When you wear the earrings, forego the bold necklace.

tip *To cut multiple pieces of chain to the same length, first cut one piece to the length you want. String the cut chain on a head pin. String the rest of the chains on the head pin. Then, trim them to the same length as the first piece.*

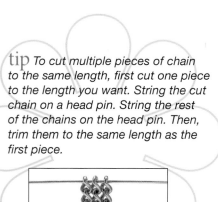

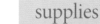

supplies
- **5** 22mm Lucite rings (The Beadin' Path)
- 8–10mm accent bead
- 2–3 in. (5–7.6cm) chain, 5–6mm links
- 22–25 in. (56–64cm) chain, 4–5mm links
- 6 in. (15cm) chain, 3–4mm links
- 1½-in. (3.8cm) head pin
- **9** 3–4mm jump rings
- lobster claw clasp
- chainnose pliers
- roundnose pliers
- diagonal wire cutters
- additional pair of chainnose pliers (optional)

Knot beads on a long ribbon

If you wood

Wooden beads often have large holes, so thicker strands, like ribbon, can fit through them. Dress up simple wood beads by knotting them on colorful silk ribbons. If you like symmetry, wear the necklace with the bow at the back of your neck. Or, for a pretty accent, wear the bow off to one side.

1 About 12 in. (30cm) from one end of a ribbon, tie an overhand knot (see Basics, p. 14).

2 String a wood bead and tie an overhand knot next to it. Repeat until there is 1 in. (2.5cm) of ribbon left. As you tie each knot, pull the ribbon taut so the necklace doesn't stretch out later.

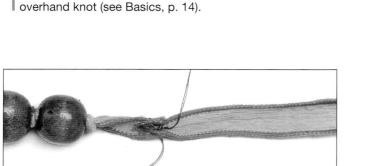

3 Thread a needle with a 12-in. (30cm) piece of thread. Attach the ribbon end to another ribbon end by sewing the two pieces together. (I used brown thread for the photo, but thread that matches the ribbon color won't show.) Trim the extra thread.

4 Repeat steps 2 and 3 until the beaded part of the necklace is within 2 in. (5cm) of the length you want your necklace to be. (My necklace is 43 in./1.1m.) Tie the ends into a bow.

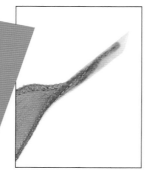

tip *Before stringing, roll a small piece of tape tightly around the end of your ribbon. Cut the tape on a slant, being careful not to cut the ribbon. You'll be able to string the taped ribbon through the beads more easily.*

supplies

- **50–60** 18–20mm wood beads with 4–5mm holes (Family Glass)
- **3** 1-yd. (.9m) ribbons, ⅝ in. (1.6cm) wide (Da Beads)
- thread in a color to match the ribbon
- sewing needle

Wear a pastel necklace in different ways

Pretty in pink

Every girl needs a lightweight, super-long necklace to wrap to her heart's content. I chose pinks that remind me of jelly beans and bubble gum for mine. To make sure the candy colors didn't get too sweet, I added gunmetal-colored spacers and chain. The chain also keeps the necklace from being too bulky.

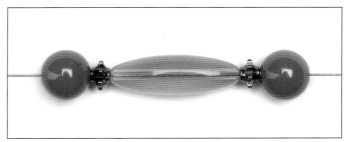

1 Decide how long you want the beaded part of your necklace to be. (My necklace is 51 in./1.3m, with a 33½-in./85.2cm beaded section and a 17½-in./44.5cm chain.) Add 6 in. (15cm) and cut a piece of beading wire to that length. On the wire, center an 8mm round bead, a 10mm oval bead, a spacer, a 16mm oval, a spacer, a 10mm oval, and an 8mm round.

2 On each end, string a 10mm round, a spacer, a rice-shaped bead, a spacer, and a 10mm round. Repeat the patterns from steps 1 and 2 until the strand is about two-thirds the length you want.

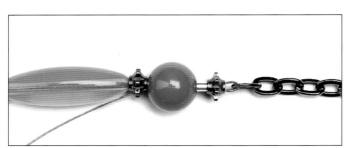

3 Cut a 16–20-in. (41–51cm) piece of chain. On one end of the beading wire, string a crimp bead, a spacer, and the chain. Go back through the last few beads strung and tighten the wire. Make a folded crimp (see Basics, p. 14). Slide the spacer over the finished crimp.

4 On the other end of the wire, string a crimp bead, a spacer, and a soldered jump ring. Finish as in step 3.

5 Check the fit, and trim links from the chain if you need to. Open a 3–4mm jump ring (Basics). Attach a lobster claw clasp and the chain. Close the jump ring.

supplies

- **8–10** 26mm rice-shaped Lucite beads (all Lucite beads from The Beadin' Path)
- **7–9** 16mm oval Lucite beads
- **14–18** 10mm oval Lucite beads
- **16–20** 10mm round Lucite beads
- **14–18** 8mm round Lucite beads
- **30–40** 5mm spacers (Vintaj)
- flexible beading wire, .014 or .015
- 16–20 in. (41–51cm) chain, 5–6mm links (Ornamentea)
- 3–4mm jump ring
- 2 crimp beads
- lobster claw clasp and soldered jump ring
- crimping pliers
- diagonal wire cutters

tip *Oxidizing metal will give it a darker finish. To oxidize chain, spacers, and findings, you can use liver of sulfur or Black Max. Both products are available from Rio Grande. Follow the instructions carefully. (If you're not sure how to do it, ask a responsible adult.)*

Cluster pearls and crystals on a fun chain necklace

Bubbly baubles

This bright necklace shows off a cascade of round and faceted beads. Since the beads are bigger than the chain links, they crowd together in a colorful display. Pick a chain strong enough to hold about 50 beads. Even though the wrapped loops may take a little time, you'll love the pretty results.

tip *It's easier to get started on this necklace if you buy a strand of mixed pearls (try Pearlwear). Then, find other beads and crystals to play up the colors in the strand.*

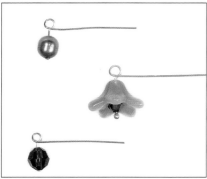

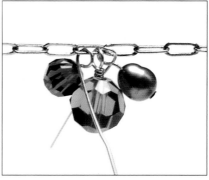

1 On a head pin, string a bead. Make the first half of a wrapped loop (see Basics, p. 14). Make 50 to 70 dangles, using pearls, crystals, and other beads.

2 Decide how long you want your necklace to be. (Mine is 17 in./ 43cm.) Cut a piece of chain to that length. Attach a bead unit to the chain's center link and complete the wraps.

3 Attach two more bead units to the center link. Complete the wraps.

4 Attach two bead units to each of the links on each side of the center.

5 Continue attaching pairs of bead units to chain links until the beaded part of the necklace is the length you want it to be. (The beaded part of my necklace is 4½ in./11.4cm.)

supplies

- **20–40** 5–10mm crystals and beads
- 16-in. (41cm) strand 5–10mm pearls
- 15–18 in. (38–46cm) chain, 4–5mm links
- **50–70** 1½-in. (3.8cm) 24-gauge head pins
- 2 4–5mm jump rings
- toggle clasp
- chainnose pliers
- roundnose pliers
- diagonal wire cutters

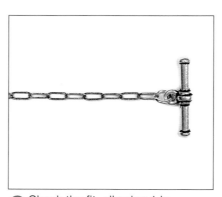

6 Check the fit, allowing 1 in. (2.5cm) for the clasp. Trim an equal amount of chain from each end, if you need to. On each end, open a jump ring (Basics). Attach half of the clasp and close the jump ring.

another project
Now that you're good at making wrapped loops, make a quick pair of earrings by attaching bead units to decorative earring wires.

Citrine and cherry quartz beads make for a cheery necklace

Sunshine state

Strung in colors that symbolize joy and warmth, this yellow and pinkish-orange necklace is perfect for a summer outfit. The necklace combines elements that are slightly different but close enough to work well together. To unify the look, choose a briolette pendant to match the shorter strand, but string it on the longer strand.

1 Decide how long you want your necklace to be. Add 6 in. (15 cm), and cut a piece of beading wire to that length (see Basics, p. 14). (My necklace is 15½ in./39.4cm.) Cut a second piece 2 in. (5cm) longer than the first piece. On the shorter wire, string nuggets until the strand is within 2 in. (5cm) of the length you want.

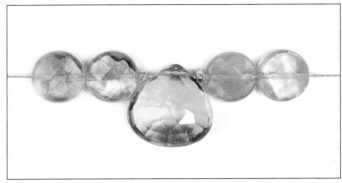

2 Center a spacer, a briolette, and a spacer on the longer wire. String coin-shaped beads on each end until the strand is within 2 in. (5cm) of the length you want.

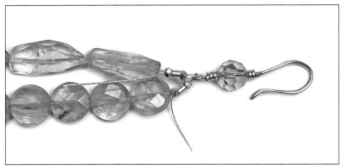

3 On each end, string a spacer, a crimp bead, a spacer, and half of the clasp. (If you like, make your own clasp – see p. 40). Check the fit (Basics). Go back through the beads just strung and tighten the wire. Crimp the crimp beads (Basics) and trim the extra wire.

supplies

- 15–20mm briolette
- 16-in. (41cm) strand 15–20mm nuggets
- 16-in. (41cm) strand 10–14mm coin-shaped beads
- **10** 3–4mm spacers

- flexible beading wire, .014 or .015
- **4** crimp beads
- hook-and-eye clasp
- chainnose pliers or crimping pliers
- diagonal wire cutters

tip *If you need to make the necklace just a little longer, string more spacers or 4mm crystals in a matching color.*

another project Make a quick pair of earrings by using a 4–5mm jump ring to attach a top-drilled crystal to the loop of an earring post. I used 8mm Swarovski bicone crystals in style #6301.

Shape your own clasp

Custom finish

A handmade hook-and-eye clasp pulls together your jewelry design by using a bead that works with your necklace. Use accent beads that match your piece, or, for a simpler look, skip the beads and just use wire.

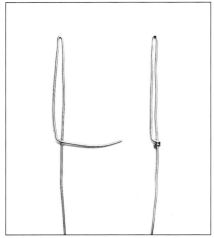

1 To make the hook half of the clasp, cut a 6-in. (15cm) piece of wire. Bend it in half. Bend one wire over the other 1¼ in. (3.2cm) from the fold. Wrap the short wire around the stem. Trim the extra wire.

2 String an accent bead and make a wrapped loop (see Basics, p. 14). Using chainnose pliers, pinch together the wires above the accent bead.

3 Bend the folded wires around a pen barrel to form a hook.

4 Using chainnose pliers, bend the tip of the hook upward.

5 To make the eye half of the clasp, cut a 3½-in. (8.9cm) piece of wire. Make a wrapped loop on one end. String an accent bead and make a 5–6mm wrapped loop. (The hook half of the clasp has to fit through this loop.)

supplies
- **2** 6–12mm accent beads
- 9½ in. (24.1cm) 18- or 20- gauge half-hard wire
- chainnose pliers
- roundnose pliers
- diagonal wire cutters

tip *The accent bead you choose determines the length of the clasp. Keep the length of the clasp in mind when stringing your necklace, and plan that it will take up 2–3 in. (5–7.6cm).*

BRACELETS

Big and bold or dainty and delicate – bracelets may be your most versatile accessory. Don't think of them as just a necklace's sidekick. Make a statement with the flick of your wrist. Try layering a beaded bracelet with a charm bracelet or a couple of bangles. If you wear a huge bracelet, wear a simple necklace or just skip it. In this chapter you'll learn how to:

- Wrap beads on suede for a quick bracelet (p. 46)
- String a chunky cuff with organic beads (p. 50)
- Hammer your own silver bangles (p. 56)
- Create a charm bracelet from vintage finds (p. 59)

Rock on

When I bought these green amethyst nuggets, I tried stringing them with different beads: seed beads, crystals, and spacers. Nothing looked quite right. Next, I tried adding a chain with heavy links, then looping a fine-link chain around the beads — both interesting, but not what I was looking for. After all my efforts, here it is: just the nuggets, with an angular clasp to complement their facets. Sometimes, a great strand of rocks doesn't need much more to become wearable jewelry.

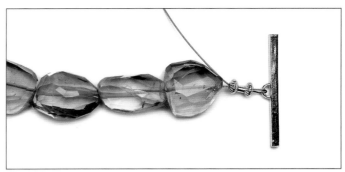

1 Cut a piece of beading wire (see Basics, p. 14). String nuggets until the strand is within 1¹/₂ in. (3.8cm) of the length you want.

2 On each end, string a spacer, a crimp bead, a spacer, and half of the clasp. Check the fit (Basics). Go back through the beads just strung and tighten the wire. Crimp the crimp beads (Basics) and trim the extra wire.

supplies

- 8-in. (20cm) strand 15–25mm nuggets (Ritual Adornments)
- **4** 3–5mm spacers
- flexible beading wire, .018 or .019
- **2** crimp beads
- toggle clasp (Saki Silver)
- chainnose pliers or crimping pliers
- diagonal wire cutters

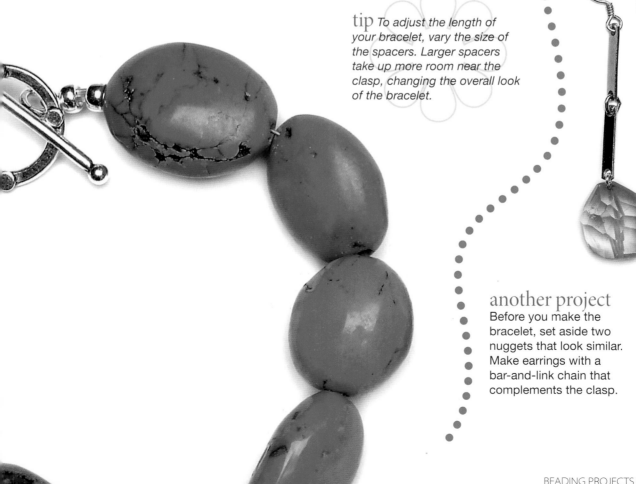

tip *To adjust the length of your bracelet, vary the size of the spacers. Larger spacers take up more room near the clasp, changing the overall look of the bracelet.*

another project

Before you make the bracelet, set aside two nuggets that look similar. Make earrings with a bar-and-link chain that complements the clasp.

Attach beads to suede for a simple cuff

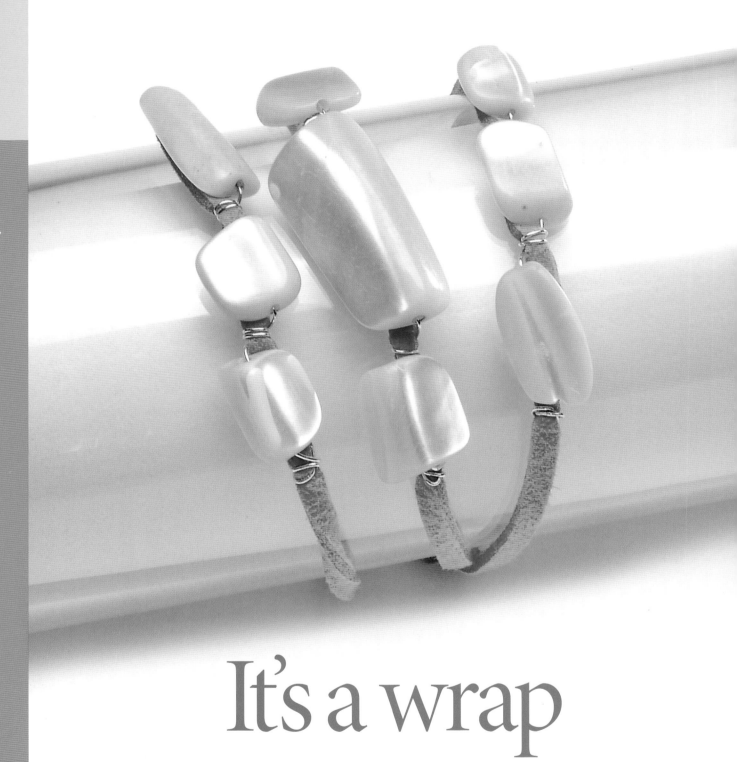

It's a wrap

Display a collection of pretty beads on a piece of bright suede,
then wrap it around your wrist for a cuff bracelet. A magnetic
clasp makes it easy to put the bracelet on and take it off.

1 Wrap a piece of suede lace around your wrist three or four times. Mark a small dot on the center of each wrap. (You'll cover the dots with beads.)

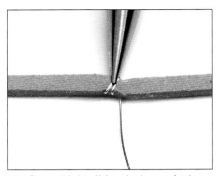

2 Cut a 12-in. (30cm) piece of wire. With chainnose pliers, push one end of the wire into the suede about 1 in. (2.5cm) from a dot. Wrap the wire around the suede two or three times.

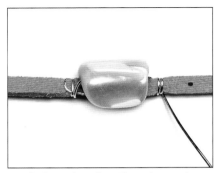

3 String a bead on the wire, and wrap the wire around the suede two or three times.

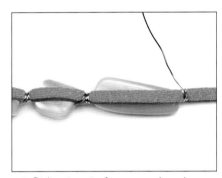

4 String two to four more beads, wrapping the wire between each bead. After the last bead, wrap the wire twice and tuck the end under a wrap on the back of the bracelet. Trim the extra wire.

5 Repeat steps 2–4 two or three more times. Check the fit, and trim each end so that the suede is 1 in. (2.5cm) short of the length you want. On each end, attach a crimp end and flatten the center (crimp portion) with chainnose pliers.

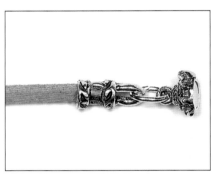

6 Open a jump ring (see Basics, p. 14), attach half of a magnetic clasp to a crimp end's loop, and close the jump ring. Repeat on the other end.

supplies

- **9–20** 6–25mm beads
- **6–20** 4–9mm spacers (optional)
- 21–32 in. (53–81cm) suede lace, 3mm width (Bead Needs, LLC)
- 3–4 ft. (.9–1.2m) 26-gauge wire
- **2** 4–5mm jump rings
- **2** crimp ends (Rio Grande)
- magnetic clasp (Fire Mountain Gems)
- chainnose pliers
- roundnose pliers
- diagonal wire cutters

tip *You can buy 26-gauge wire at craft stores like Jo-Ann or Michaels. Try including colored craft wire as a design element in your bracelet.*

In your own words

Whatever you've got to say, express it with a colorful set
of stretch bracelets. Spell out a nickname or favorite saying;
you can even divide the message between different bracelets.
By using Czech fire-polished beads — maybe in your school
colors — a whole armful of bracelets will cost just a few dollars.
Of course, if you're a girl of few words, skip the message,
and you'll still have a pretty set of baubles.

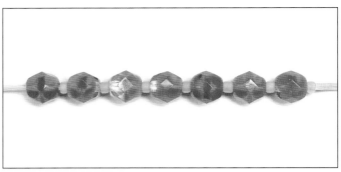

1 Cut a 9–11-in. (23–28cm) piece of ribbon elastic. For beads with holes that can handle a doubled thickness of elastic, cut an 18–22-in. (46–56cm) piece. Thread a twisted-wire beading needle with the ribbon elastic and tape the end(s). On your workspace, arrange alphabet beads to form words. Measure the total length of the words.

2 Decide how long you want your bracelet to be. Subtract the length of the words, and then divide that number in half. String that length of fire-polished beads (and 11º seed beads, if you like) on the elastic. End with an 11º. (If the math is confusing, just make sure to leave room for the alphabet beads.)

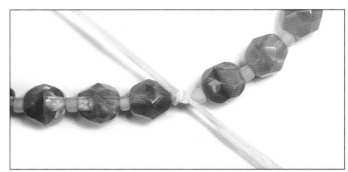

3 String the alphabet beads to form words. String an 11º between and after each word.

4 String fire-polished beads and 11ºs until the bracelet is the length you want. Check the fit. If you need to, remove beads from the taped end or string beads on the needle end. Tie a surgeon's knot (see Basics, p. 14). Apply glue to the knot and trim the ends to ⅛ in. (3mm). Gently stretch the bracelet to hide the knot inside a bead.

supplies

The supply list and instructions are for a bracelet with alphabet beads. For a bracelet without alphabet beads, you can use 3–6mm beads or 6º, 8º, or 11º seed beads.
- **3–12** 6mm alphabet beads (Shipwreck Beads)
- **15–20** 6mm Czech fire-polished beads
- **15–20** 11º seed beads
- ribbon elastic
- G-S Hypo Cement
- twisted-wire beading needle

tip *Don't have a twisted-wire beading needle? You can make your own: Cut a 4-in. (10cm) piece of .010 flexible beading wire and fold it in half. Loop the ribbon elastic through the fold and string beads over the ends of the wire and onto the elastic.*

Make an easy memory-wire cuff

Natural-material girl

Memory wire is a coiled wire (it looks like a Slinky®) that keeps its shape. It comes in necklace and ring sizes, but I especially love it for bracelets because cuffs will spring back to their original shape. Even though I chose wood, bamboo, and rudraksha seeds for this easy wraparound bracelet, you can use other beads. Just make sure the bead holes are large enough to fit over the wire.

1 Separate five or six memory-wire coils from the stack. Cut the memory wire with heavy-duty wire cutters. Using roundnose pliers, make a small loop on one end.

2 String three small wood beads, alternating them with a rudraksha bead, a bamboo bead, and a large wood bead. Repeat until the bracelet is the length you want, ending with a small wood bead.

3 Check the fit, and add or remove beads if you need to. Cut the memory wire $3/8$ in. (1cm) from the last bead. Make a loop on the end of the wire.

tip *If you don't have heavy-duty wire cutters, here's another way you can cut memory wire: Hold the wire with chainnose pliers and bend it back and forth at one place until it breaks. Don't use jewelry-weight cutters; memory wire will ruin the blades.*

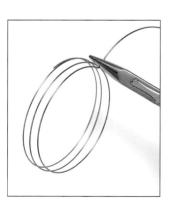

supplies
- **11–15** 16mm wood beads (all beads from Eclectica)
- **12–16** 12–15mm bamboo beads
- **12–16** 12–14mm rudraksha beads
- 16-in. (41cm) strand 5–6mm round wood beads
- memory wire, bracelet (2 in./5cm) diameter
- chainnose pliers
- roundnose pliers
- heavy-duty wire cutters (optional)

Link beads and jump rings in fresh colors

Enjoy the greenery

Using plain loops, connect green beads and hammered silver links for a fun and simple bracelet. Vintage Lucite and crystals in kelly, jade, light green, and yellow green make this an ideal springtime accessory.

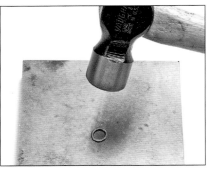

1 Cut a 1¼-in. (3.2cm) piece of wire. Make a plain loop (see Basics, p. 14) at one end. String a 12mm bead and make a plain loop. Repeat to make 11 to 15 bead units, using 8–9mm, 10mm, and 12mm beads.

2 On a bench block or anvil, hammer a 9–10mm jump ring. Flip the jump ring over and hammer the other side. Repeat with the rest of the 9–10mm jump rings.

3 Open each loop (Basics) of a 12mm-bead unit. Attach a hammered jump ring to one loop and a 10mm-bead unit to the other loop. Close the loops. Attach a hammered jump ring to the remaining loop of the 10mm-bead unit. Attach a 10mm-bead unit in a second color to the hammered jump ring and an 8mm-bead unit to the last loop. Repeat until the bracelet is within ½ in. (1.3cm) of the length you want.

4 Check the fit, and add or remove bead units or hammered jump rings if you need to. Make sure there is a hammered jump ring on one end. String a 10mm bead on a head pin. Make a plain loop. Open the loop and attach a bead unit. Close the loop. Attach the dangle to one end.

5 Open a 4–5mm jump ring (Basics). Attach a lobster claw clasp to the other end, and close the jump ring.

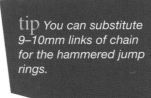

tip *You can substitute 9–10mm links of chain for the hammered jump rings.*

supplies
- **3–4** 12mm beads
- **6–8** 10mm beads, in two colors
- **3–4** 8–9mm beads
- 13–15 in. (33–38cm) 20- or 22-gauge half-hard wire
- 1½-in. (3.8cm) head pin
- **5–7** 9–10mm soldered sterling silver jump rings (Rio Grande)
- 4–5mm jump ring
- lobster claw clasp
- chainnose pliers
- roundnose pliers
- diagonal wire cutters
- bench block or anvil
- hammer

another project
Make a fun pair of earrings using leftover beads from the bracelet and some chain (see p. 66).

Highlight one element on a chain bracelet

Chainy days

When you want to feature a single bead or charm, try a quick chain bracelet. Look at how big the links are compared to the bead, and figure out how visible you want the chain to be. An art bead might look good on a finer chain, while a decorative clasp would pair well with a chunky chain.

tip *If you like, you can use a toggle clasp instead of a lobster claw clasp. Just make sure you're using a heavy enough chain (the weight helps keep the clasp closed).*

design idea Showcase a padlock clasp with large-link chain for a bold bracelet. (The clasp is from Rio Grande; the chain is from Ornamentea.)

1 Cut a piece of chain 1 in. (2.5cm) shorter than the length you want your bracelet to be. Open a 3–4mm jump ring (see Basics, p. 14). Attach a lobster claw clasp to one end. Close the jump ring. Repeat on the other end, using a soldered jump ring in place of the clasp.

2 Cut a 3½-in. (8.9cm) piece of wire. String a bead and make a set of wraps above it (Basics). Make the first half of a wrapped loop (Basics) above the wraps, perpendicular to the bead.

3 Attach the dangle to the soldered jump ring. Complete the wraps.

supplies
- 15–25mm focal bead (leaf bead from Lisa Kan Designs)
- 6–8 in. (15–20cm) chain, 9–14mm links
- 3½ in. (8.9cm) 22- or 24-gauge half-hard wire
- **2** 3–4mm jump rings
- lobster claw clasp and soldered jump ring
- chainnose pliers
- roundnose pliers
- diagonal wire cutters

Encircle a premade bracelet with pearls

Mix & match

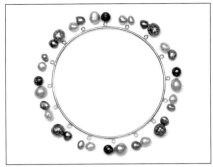

1 On your workspace, arrange two pearls next to one loop on a bangle. (We'll call this the first loop.) Arrange a matching pair next to the fifth, ninth, and thirteenth loops. Continue arranging pairs of pearls (in different color combinations) so each is across from a matching pair.

2 String a pearl on a head pin, and make the first half of a wrapped loop (see Basics, p. 14). Make a second dangle with the other pearl in that pair.

If you have extra pearls left over from projects, this bangle bracelet is a great way to use them. Different pearl styles (like round, rice, and faceted pearls) look pretty together in this dainty bracelet. Pair different colors next to each other for contrast.

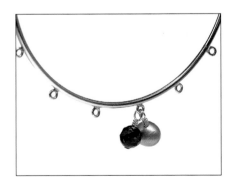

3 Attach the pair of dangles to the corresponding loop on the bangle. Complete the wraps. Repeat with the rest of the pearls.

tip *For a quicker bangle, attach only one pearl to each loop. Each bead will stand out more.*

supplies

- **32** 4–8mm pearls, **4** each in eight colors
- bangle bracelet with 16 loops (Rings & Things)
- **32** 1½-in. (3.8cm) head pins
- chainnose pliers
- roundnose pliers
- diagonal wire cutters

Crystals orbit silver wire in an armful of bangles

Celestial circles

Hammering hardens a wire, helping it maintain its shape while also giving it a softer, matte finish. Flecked with sparkling crystals, these bangles provide dazzling opportunities: Wear a stack to glam it up, or put on one or two for easy accessorizing.

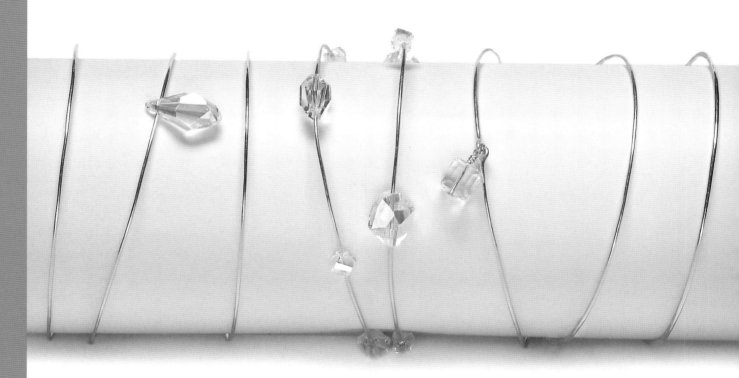

1 Cut an 8–9-in. (20–23cm) piece of wire. Wrap it around the base of a drinking glass (about 8½ in./21.6cm in diameter) so the ends overlap slightly.

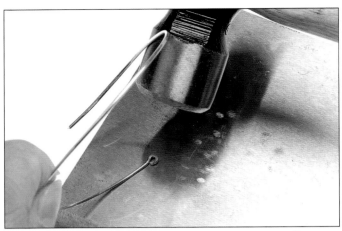

2 Make a plain loop (see Basics, p. 14) on one end. If you like, hammer the loop on a bench block or anvil.

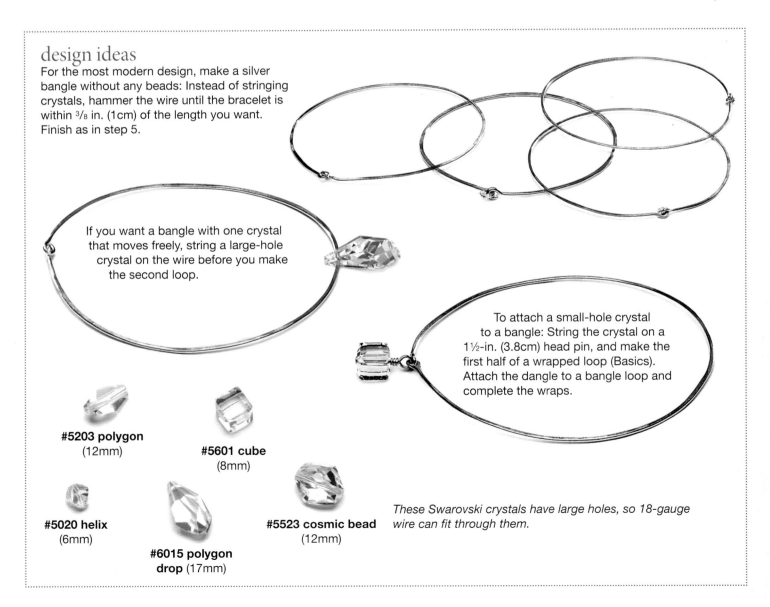

design ideas

For the most modern design, make a silver bangle without any beads: Instead of stringing crystals, hammer the wire until the bracelet is within ³⁄₈ in. (1cm) of the length you want. Finish as in step 5.

If you want a bangle with one crystal that moves freely, string a large-hole crystal on the wire before you make the second loop.

To attach a small-hole crystal to a bangle: String the crystal on a 1½-in. (3.8cm) head pin, and make the first half of a wrapped loop (Basics). Attach the dangle to a bangle loop and complete the wraps.

#5203 polygon
(12mm)

#5601 cube
(8mm)

#5020 helix
(6mm)

#6015 polygon drop (17mm)

#5523 cosmic bead
(12mm)

These Swarovski crystals have large holes, so 18-gauge wire can fit through them.

Crystals orbit silver wire in an armful of bangles

tip *If you like, use 16-gauge wire for plain bangles.*

3 String a crystal. Position the wire so the crystal hangs off the bench block or anvil. Hammer 1–1½ in. (2.5–3.8cm) of the wire next to the crystal. Flip the bracelet over and hammer the other side.

4 Continue stringing crystals and hammering sections of wire until the bracelet is within ³/₈ in. (1cm) of the length you want. Trim the wire, if you need to.

5 Make a plain loop on the end, perpendicular to the first loop. Open the second loop (Basics) and attach it to the first. Close the loop.

supplies

(for each bracelet)
- **1–5** 6–18mm Swarovski crystals (JewelrySupply.com)
- 8–9 in. (20–23cm) 18-gauge half-hard round wire (Fire Mountain Gems)
- 1½-in. (3.8cm) head pin (optional, for dangle)
- chainnose pliers
- roundnose pliers
- diagonal wire cutters
- hammer
- bench block or anvil
- drinking glass

Flaunt your interests with a unique charm bracelet

Charmed

For a fun, personal accessory, nothing beats a charm bracelet. Traditional bracelets have charms that say something about you: mine have dogs and tennis racquets (I love both). If you like vintage stuff, scour local thrift stores or buy jewelry grab bags online. Don't be afraid to use oversized charms like the Bingo Nut charm shown here. Bigger can be better.

Flaunt your interests with a unique charm bracelet

supplies

- **15–30** charms, post earrings, and clip earrings
- **8–15** 7–12mm accent beads
- **8–30** 3–12mm spacers or bead caps (optional)
- 7–8 in. (18–20cm) chain, 9–14mm links (Chelsea's Beads)
- **8–15** 1½-in. (3.8cm) 22-gauge head pins
- **17–32** 5–6mm oval jump rings
- 3–4mm jump rings for charms with small loops
- toggle clasp
- chainnose pliers
- roundnose pliers
- diagonal wire cutters
- metal file or emery board
- additional pair of chainnose pliers (optional)
- heavy-duty wire cutters (optional)

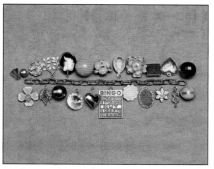

1 Cut a piece of chain to the length you want your bracelet to be. On your workspace, arrange the charms and earrings along the chain. Balance different colors, shapes, sizes, and textures, using accent beads to fill in gaps.

2 Make earrings into charms. For a post earring: Use roundnose pliers to bend the earring wire into a loop (see Basics, p. 14). Don't overwork the wire; it may be brittle. Repeat with the clip earrings, after trimming the hinged part of the clip. File any jagged edges.

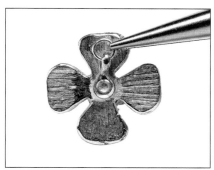

3 If a charm has a small loop or a loop in the center, use a jump ring so it hangs better. Open a 3–4mm jump ring (Basics). Attach the charm's loop and close the jump ring.

4 Open an oval jump ring. Attach a charm to the center chain link. Close the jump ring. (I usually put the largest charm in the center, where it offsets the size of the clasp.)

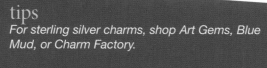

tips

For sterling silver charms, shop Art Gems, Blue Mud, or Charm Factory.

Shop online auctions like eBay or Goodwill for vintage jewelry. (Type in "jewelry lots" to search. "Lots" are groups of things, often sold by weight.) Check what quantity the seller is offering; I like to order at least three or four pounds so I have lots of stuff to look through. Also, don't forget about shipping when figuring out your bid — it can add a lot to the total cost.

5 Open the loop of a post-earring charm and attach it to the chain. Close the loop. Working outward from the center, attach the rest of the post-earring charms. Use oval jump rings to attach the rest of the charms to the chain.

6 On a head pin, string an accent bead, plus spacers or bead caps, if you want. Make the first half of a wrapped loop (Basics). Repeat with the rest of the accent beads. Attach each bead unit to the chain and complete the wraps.

7 Check the fit, and trim links from the chain if you need to. Use an oval jump ring to attach half of the clasp to each end. If you like, attach a charm or a bead to the loop half of the clasp.

design ideas

Pearl bracelet Use just one type of bead and charms to make a dressy bracelet. When I fished this bracelet out of a tangle of junk jewelry, it had just three clamshell charms. I stayed true to the original design by attaching a pearl to each link. To play up the costume-y feel, I used faux — mostly glass and vintage — pearls.

Silver bracelet Make a charm bracelet for a friend using charms with personal meaning. This was a gift for Katy, my friend since third grade. When we met, she was holding her cat — see the cat charm? I included the clarinet to remind her of playing in our high school band, and the desk represents her career as a teacher.

Gold bracelet Use a variety of fun jewelry components to make an original bracelet. All of these charms came from a Goodwill grab bag of jewelry. I used goldtone button covers, post earrings, and pendants, and then included pearls and crystals in bright colors.

EARRINGS

Earrings are fast and easy to make, so it's simple to create a pair for any outfit. After years of not being able to wear cute earrings, I finally went to the mall with my friend and got my ears pierced. I'm so glad I did! Whether you've got a huge collection of earrings, just got your ears pierced, or need a quick gift, there's something satisfying about making your own earrings. They're also a great way to use those last few beads from a strand. Here are some of the things you'll learn to do:

- Put together colorful little bead clusters (p. 66)
- Attach beads to pre-made earring findings (p. 70)
- Turn sparkling crystals into dangling chandeliers (p. 78)
- Hammer some giant hoops (p. 80)

Drop everything

To make basic earrings, you need to do only three simple things: String beads on a head pin, make a loop, and attach an earring wire. These easy earrings are a pretty way to use leftover beads. I used gemstone ovals and pearls and crystals, but just about any combination of beads (and spacers, if you like) lends itself to a drop. It's so easy, you'll make a pair for all of your favorite outfits.

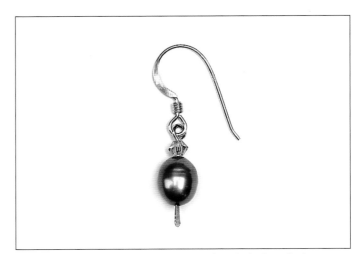

1 On a head pin (to make your own, see below), string beads and spacers however you want. Make a plain loop or a wrapped loop (see Basics, p. 14).

2 Open the loop of an earring wire (Basics). Attach the dangle and close the loop. Make a second earring to match the first.

supplies

- **2 or more** 4–12mm beads
- **2 or more** 3–6mm spacers (optional)
- **2** 1½-in. (3.8cm) head pins
- pair of earring wires or posts
- chainnose pliers
- roundnose pliers
- diagonal wire cutters

tip *If the bottom bead has a large hole, use a head pin with a decorative end, or string a seed bead or a spacer before stringing the bead.*

design ideas

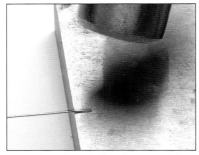

To make a head pin with a paddle on the end, cut a piece of 22- or 24-gauge round wire. On a bench block or anvil, hammer the tip of the wire. File the edges if they're sharp.

Try using head pins in decorative or jeweled styles. These head pins are from Fire Mountain Gems and JewelrySupply.com.

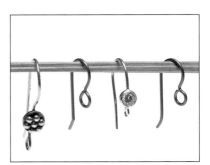

You can get earring wires in other metals or use embellished earring findings. From left to right: Bali silver (Rupa B. Designs), natural brass (Vintaj), cubic zirconia (House of Gems), and niobium (Rings & Things).

Cute clusters

These super-easy earrings use only one technique — making plain loops — to dangle three beads from a chain. The bead shape, chain, and earring wire you choose create the overall effect. Whether you like chunky clusters or delicate dangles, you can achieve different looks by varying the basic earring.

1 On a head pin, string a bead. Make a plain loop (see Basics, p. 14). Make two more bead units.

2 Cut a piece of chain to the length you want. (The chains on these earrings are ½ in./1.3cm.) Open the loop of an earring wire (Basics) and attach the chain. Close the loop.

3 Open the loop (Basics) of the largest bead unit. Attach it to the bottom chain link and close the loop.

4 Attach two other bead units to the next links on opposite sides of the chain. If you like, trim links from the top of the dangle and reattach it to the earring wire. Make a second earring as the mirror image of the first.

supplies

- **6** 4–12mm beads
- 1–2 in. (2.5–5cm) cable chain, 3–5mm links
- **6** 1½-in. (3.8cm) head pins
- pair of earring wires
- chainnose pliers
- roundnose pliers
- diagonal wire cutters

tip *Attach each chain to an earring wire before attaching the bead units. It will be easier to handle the short pieces of chain when you're attaching the cluster.*

design ideas

For the basic cluster, I went for an antique look with muted colors and gold findings. The earrings combine matte finish and sparkle, smooth and faceted textures, and opaque and transparent beads. So that it doesn't overwhelm the other beads, the largest bead (12mm) is the least colorful.

Use a hammered 9–10mm jump ring in place of the bottom bead in the cluster. Use a 3–4mm jump ring to attach the jump ring to the chain.

For long, linear earrings, skip the chain. Instead, attach the cluster directly to the loop of an earring thread (available from Rings & Things). Also, use smaller beads (I used 4mm, 6mm, and 8mm sizes).

For fuller earrings, attach five or more bead units to the chain. My earrings have 4–8mm round, rondelle, and coin-shaped gemstones and crystals on a 3mm cable chain. The smaller the chain link, the closer together the beads will hang.

Tourmaline beads make for dynamic earrings

Dotted lines

Although you can use any gemstone for these long earrings, tourmaline beads show a graduated effect since individual beads have multiple colors. This pair of earrings boasts shades of pink, green, and a combination of the two. Buy a strand and pair the beads in different ways: pinks and browns, yellow-greens and olives, or grays and blue-greens. Some tourmaline shapes can be pricey, but a strand of simple ovals can cost less than $25.

1 Choose five pairs of oval beads in a range of colors. Set aside one group. On a head pin, string a crystal. Make a plain loop (see Basics, p. 14).

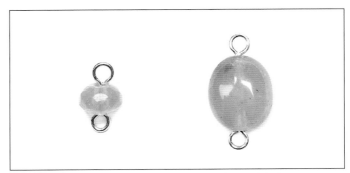

2 Cut a 1-in. (2.5cm) piece of wire. Make a plain loop on one end. String a rondelle and make a plain loop. Repeat with five oval beads, using 1¼-in. (3.2cm) pieces of wire.

3 Open one loop (Basics) of the rondelle unit. Attach the lightest-colored oval unit and close the loop. Continue attaching oval units in order from lightest to darkest. End with the crystal unit.

4 Open the loop of an earring post (Basics) and attach the dangle. Close the loop. Make a second earring to match the first.

supplies

- 16-in. (41cm) strand 5–9mm oval tourmaline beads (Rio Grande)
- 2 5–10mm coin-shaped or oval crystals
- 2 4–5mm faceted rondelles
- 15 in. (38cm) 24-gauge half-hard wire
- 2 1½-in. (3.8cm) head pins
- pair of earring posts with ear nuts
- chainnose pliers
- roundnose pliers
- diagonal wire cutters

tip *The green-and-pink earrings are 3½ in. (8.9cm) long. If you want shorter earrings, use fewer beads in each earring. (This pair is 2 in./5cm long.) Or, for daintier earrings, use 4–5mm tourmaline rondelles instead of the ovals and skip the crystals.*

Hip hoops

Since crystals come in so many fabulous hues, it's easy to show a range of colors in one pair of earrings. There's also a huge variety of hoops, in lots of sizes and with different arrangements of loops. Indulge in a few kinds to figure out what style you like best.

1 On a head pin, string a round crystal. Make the first half of a wrapped loop (see Basics, p. 14). Repeat with six rondelles (two each of three colors).

2 Attach the round-crystal unit to the bottom center loop of an earring hoop. Complete the wraps.

3 Attach rondelle units to the rest of the loops, from darkest to lightest.

4 Open the loop of an earring wire (Basics). Attach the dangle and close the loop. Make a second earring to match the first.

supplies

- **2** 6mm round crystals
- **12** 5mm faceted rondelles, **4** each of three colors
- **14** 1½-in. (3.8cm) head pins
- pair of earring hoops with seven loops (Artbeads.com)
- pair of earring wires
- chainnose pliers
- roundnose pliers
- diagonal wire cutters

tip *If you attach a mix of beads, make sure the earrings are mirror images of each other (not two of the same).*

design idea

Try small hoop findings with a loop in the center. I used shades of green for an earthy, bohemian look.

Finding
your way

Metal charms and findings give you lots of design options.
Here are a couple of quick ways to showcase them in
earrings: To make the charms stand out, display them against
a flat background bead in a contrasting color. Or, create a
vintage feel by dangling a crystal briolette from the bottom.
Either way, you'll have a pair of earrings in a matter of minutes.

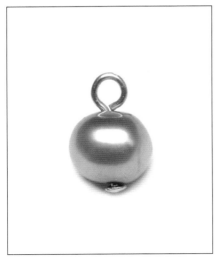

1 **shell-and-pearl earrings** On a head pin, string a bead. Make a plain loop (see Basics, p. 14).

2 Open the loop (Basics). Attach the bottom loop of a charm and close the bead's loop.

3 Open the loop of an earring wire. Attach the dangle and a shell pendant. Close the loop. Make a second earring to match the first.

1 **briolette earrings** Open a jump ring. Attach a briolette to the bottom loop of a charm, and close the jump ring.

2 Open the loop of an earring wire. Attach the dangle, and close the loop. Make a second earring to match the first.

tip *With the shell earrings, have fun experimenting with different background shapes: round, oval, square, or rectangular shells also make a pretty canvas for charms.*

supplies

shell-and-pearl earrings
- **2** 16–19mm charms with two loops (dragonfly charms from Vintaj)
- **2** flat shell pendants, approximately 12 x 18mm (teardrop-shaped shells from Beads and Pieces)
- **2** 4–5mm beads
- **2** 1-in. (2.5cm) head pins
- pair of earring wires
- chainnose pliers
- roundnose pliers
- diagonal wire cutters

briolette earrings
- **2** 16–19mm charms with two loops
- **2** 11mm crystal briolettes (Fusion Beads)
- **2** 3–5mm jump rings
- pair of earring wires
- chainnose pliers
- roundnose pliers
- diagonal wire cutters

Assorted chains dangle in mixed-metal earrings

Seeing stars

You won't need heavy metals to rock these chain tassel earrings. Chains in different finishes, styles, and sizes burst from vintage star charms. If you're not into stargazing, try hearts or a flat bead to create a similar effect.

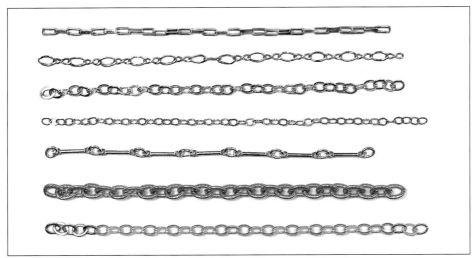

tip *Trim the chains after the earring is put together. You'll get a better view of how the lengths look.*

1 Cut pairs of five to eight different chains. (I cut my chains approximately 3 in./7.6cm long.) See p. 31 for a tip on cutting chains to the same lengths.

2 To make a dangle: Open a jump ring (see Basics, p. 14). Attach one group of chains and close the jump ring. Repeat with the second group of chains.

3 Open the loop of an earring wire (Basics). Attach a charm and a dangle. Close the loop. For the second earring, attach the dangle so it is the mirror image of the first. Trim the chains as desired.

another project Mix and match different charms in one pair of earrings. (Fortune cookie and chopstick charms are available from Shipwreck Beads.)

supplies

- **2** 7–12mm charms
- 4–8 in. (10–20cm) each of **5–8** different chains, 2–4mm links
- **2** 5–6mm oval jump rings
- pair of earring wires
- chainnose pliers
- roundnose pliers
- diagonal wire cutters

Suspend beach-themed beads and charms from chain

Natural beauties

Here's another way to use chain in earrings: Dangle pearls, crystals, and nature-themed brass charms in a pair of bountiful earrings. Consider using charms in starfish, seashell, butterfly, or dragonfly shapes — just make sure you choose two different ones for an appealing balance.

1 On a head pin, string a pearl or a crystal. Make the first half of a wrapped loop (see Basics, p. 14). Make five to nine bead units.

2 Cut a piece of chain to the length you want. (The chains in my earrings are 1⅞ in./4.8cm.) Open a jump ring (Basics), and attach a briolette to the chain. Close the jump ring.

3 Attach each bead unit to a link of chain as you like. Leave ¼ in. (6mm) of chain open at the top and ½ in. (1.3cm) open at the bottom for charms. Complete the wraps.

supplies

- **4** 8–12mm charms, **2** each of two kinds (bird and sand-dollar charms from TLS Designs)
- **2** briolettes, approximately 11mm
- **4–8** 3–5mm pearls
- **6–10** 3–4mm crystals
- **4–5** in. (10–13cm) chain, 3–4mm links
- **10–18** 1½-in. (3.8cm) 24-gauge head pins
- **4** 3–4mm jump rings
- pair of earring wires
- chainnose pliers
- roundnose pliers
- diagonal wire cutters

4 Use a jump ring to attach a large charm to a link near the bottom of the chain.

5 Open the loop of an earring wire (Basics). Attach a small charm and the dangle. Close the loop. Make the second earring as the mirror image of the first.

tip *I used Swarovski briolettes in style #6010. If a jump ring won't fit through your briolettes, attach each bead with a wrapped loop instead.*

Make dramatic earrings with crystals and briolettes

Cheers for chandeliers

Chandelier earrings light up any outfit. They can even make a T-shirt and jeans look pulled together. For these earrings, you'll make lots of plain and wrapped loops. To create the curtains of color, use 3mm, 4mm, and 5mm crystals in increasingly darker colors, ending with briolettes.

1 Cut a 3-in. (7.6cm) piece of 26-gauge wire. String a briolette and make a set of wraps above it (see Basics, p. 14). Make a wrapped loop above the wraps (Basics).

2 Cut a 1-in. (2.5cm) piece of 24-gauge wire. Make a plain loop (Basics) on one end. String a 3mm bicone crystal and make a plain loop. Repeat with a 4mm bicone and a 5mm bicone. Make five bicone units in each size.

3 Open each loop (Basics) of a 5mm-bicone unit. On one loop, attach a briolette unit; on the other, attach a 4mm-bicone unit. Close the loops. Attach a 3mm-bicone unit to the other loop of the 4mm-bicone unit. Repeat to make five dangles.

4 Open the top loop of a dangle and attach a bottom loop of a chandelier finding. Close the dangle's loop. Repeat with the four other dangles.

5 Open the loop of an earring wire (Basics) and attach the chandelier finding. Close the loop. Make a second earring to match the first.

supplies
- **10** 6–9mm briolettes
- **10** 5mm bicone crystals
- **10** 4mm bicone crystals
- **10** 3mm bicone crystals
- 30 in. (76cm) 24-gauge half-hard wire
- 30 in. (76cm) 26-gauge half-hard wire
- pair of 20–35mm chandelier findings with five loops (The Bead Shop)
- pair of earring wires
- chainnose pliers
- roundnose pliers
- diagonal wire cutters

tip *For less glitzy earrings, skip the crystals and just attach briolettes to a pair of chandelier findings.*

Playing hoops

Hoop earrings are a jewelry must-have. They're an easy way to change or accent your style. Tiny hoops sprinkled with gemstones are classics; huge hoops with charms lend bohemian flavor to a tank top and jeans. You can either attach beads with wrapped loops or string them right on the wire.

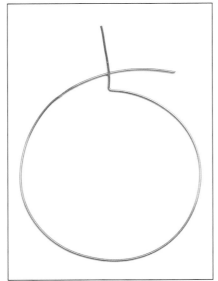

1 Cut a 7–12-in. (18–30cm) piece of 20-gauge wire. (A 12-in./30cm piece will make a bangle-sized hoop.) Wrap the wire around a round object (like a 35mm-film canister or a round tea tin). Gently press the wire into the object to make a consistent shape. About 1 in. (2.5cm) from one end, bend the wire upward to make a stem.

2 Open a 3–4mm jump ring (see Basics, p. 14). Attach a charm and close the jump ring. Repeat with a second charm. String the dangles on the wire. Wrap the longer wire around the stem and trim the extra wrapping wire.

tip *To make a consistent hoop, you can also keep the round object in place when you wrap the wire around the stem. Attach the dangles after you've made the first half of a wrapped loop.*

3 Make a plain loop (Basics) with the stem wire. Trim the extra wire.

Hammer your own hoop earrings

4 Moving the dangles out of the way, place the hoop on a bench block or anvil and hammer gently. Flip the hoop over and hammer the other side.

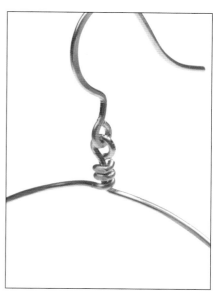

5 If you like, make your own earring wires (see p. 83). Open the loop of an earring wire (Basics) and attach the hoop. Close the loop. Make a second earring as the mirror image of the first.

design idea If you prefer a hoop without an additional earring wire, wrap the hoop wire around a round object, make a small loop at one end, and trim the wire ¼ in. (6mm) past the loop. String beads and bend the wire upward at a right angle.

Make your own earring wires

Curves ahead

Forming your own earring wires is easy, and a handmade pair will add a personal touch to your finished earrings. If you like, hammer the wires to harden them and add texture.

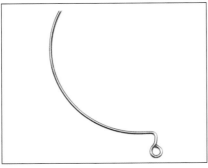

1 Cut a 2-in. (5cm) piece of wire. Make a plain loop (see Basics, p. 14). Using chainnose pliers, make a right-angle bend ⅛ in. (3mm) from the loop. If you like, add a bead before making the bend.

2 Curve the wire around a pen barrel so it forms a question-mark shape.

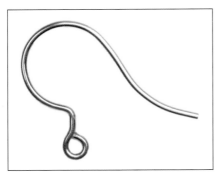

3 Remove the pen. With your fingers, curve the wire upward a little bit. Trim the extra wire.

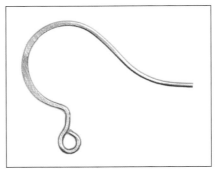

4 To add texture, hammer the wire on a bench block or anvil. Don't hammer too close to the tip (that's the part that goes in your ear). File the end. Make a second earring wire to match the first.

tip *Before using sterling silver or gold-filled wire to make your findings, practice with copper wire because it's cheaper. Keep your favorite practice earring wires as a reminder of the shape and size you're trying to make.*

supplies
- 4 in. (10cm) 20-gauge half-hard wire
- chainnose pliers
- roundnose pliers
- diagonal wire cutters
- ball-peen hammer
- bench block or anvil
- metal file or emery board

A FEW MORE IDEAS

By this point, I'm sure you're bursting with jewelry-making ideas. Maybe you've tried a few projects and have some extra beads to use up. Why not make something decorative or unusual? Try making a ring or a belt you can wear as a necklace or bracelet. With so many possibilities to choose from, I couldn't resist including a few more projects in the book. Here you'll learn to:

- Attach beads for easy stacking rings (p. 86)
- Make a colorful ring (p. 87)
- String a snowflake ornament with vintage beads (p. 88)
- Hang beads from chain in a pretty belt (p. 90)

tip *Although you can use a jump ring to attach a top-drilled bead, a wrapped loop will hold it more securely.*

Stacking up

Showcase your favorite beads on sterling silver rings. Buy a few ring findings, attach a single bead to each, and wear them together to glam up your style. You can mix textures by including a charm on one of your rings.

supplies

- **3–5** 8–15mm beads or charms
- 1½-in. (3.8cm) head pin for each bead
- 3 in. (7.6cm) 24-gauge half-hard wire for each top-drilled bead
- **3–4mm** jump ring for each charm
- **3–5** ring findings with loops (Auntie's Beads)
- chainnose pliers
- roundnose pliers
- diagonal wire cutters

1 For each bead: On a head pin, string a bead. Make the first half of a wrapped loop (see Basics, p. 14).

2 For each top-drilled bead: Cut a 3-in. (7.6cm) piece of wire. String a bead and make a set of wraps above it (Basics). Make the first half of a wrapped loop perpendicular to the bead.

3 Attach each dangle to the loop of a ring finding, and complete the wraps.

4 For each charm: Open a jump ring (Basics). Attach a charm to the loop of a ring finding. Close the jump ring.

Ring tones

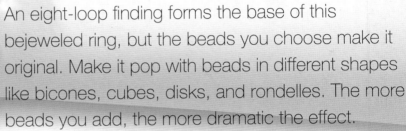

An eight-loop finding forms the base of this bejeweled ring, but the beads you choose make it original. Make it pop with beads in different shapes like bicones, cubes, disks, and rondelles. The more beads you add, the more dramatic the effect.

1 String a bead on a head pin. Make the first half of a wrapped loop (see Basics, p. 14). Repeat with the rest of the beads.

2 Attach a dangle to a loop of a ring finding. Complete the wraps.

supplies

- **12–16** 5–12mm crystals, pearls, and gemstones
- **12–16** 1½-in. (3.8cm) head pins
- ring finding with eight loops (Knot Just Beads)
- chainnose pliers
- roundnose pliers
- diagonal wire cutters

3 Attach one dangle to each of the ring's loops.

4 Try on the ring to see how the beads fall and where more can be attached. Attach the rest of the dangles.

tip *For a front-to-back-drilled bead, attach the bead to a ring loop with a 3–4mm jump ring.*

Vintage beads and crystals combine in a holiday ornament

Fabulous flakes

Beaded snowflakes are a breeze to make. To find vintage plastic, paper, glass, and wood beads, visit your local craft store or thrift store, or check on eBay. Then, combine your finds with crystals for contrast. The mix of old and new beads makes fun, one-of-a-kind ornaments that you can hang on a holiday tree. Or, give them as gifts — try pink and green for a preppy pal, black for a goth girl, or pale pearls for a friend with classic style.

1 String a 4mm crystal or a seed bead on one spoke of a snowflake form. String different beads and spacers on that spoke, leaving about ⅜ in. (1cm) uncovered. Tape the end. Repeat the pattern on the rest of the spokes, or change the pattern on every other spoke (like in the purple snowflake).

2 Remove the tape from one spoke. Use roundnose pliers to roll a loop on the end. (You can also use chainnose pliers to help squeeze the loop closed.) Repeat on the rest of the spokes.

3 String a piece of ribbon through one of the loops. Bring the ends together and tie an overhand knot (see Basics, p. 14). Trim the extra ribbon. You can also apply Dritz Fray Check to the ends to prevent fraying.

supplies

- **18–30** 5–15mm beads
- **6** 4mm crystals or **6** 11º or 8º seed beads
- **6–24** 4–8mm flat spacers
- **6** 3–4mm round spacers
- snowflake form (Knot Just Beads)
- 8 in. (20cm) ⅛–½-in. (3–13mm) wide ribbon
- chainnose pliers
- roundnose pliers
- heavy-duty wire cutters (optional)
- Dritz Fray Check (optional)

tip *Metal snowflake forms have stiff spokes. String a round spacer as the last bead on each spoke so you don't break the beads when you make a loop. Also, don't worry if your loops aren't round — no one will notice!*

Hip adornment

Sling a jeweled chain around your favorite pair of jeans,
or wear it as a long necklace or a wraparound
bracelet. If you like your jewelry a bit edgier,
use a larger-link chain and
bigger beads.

1 To make a dangle, string a bead on a head pin. Make the first half of a wrapped loop (see Basics, p. 14). Make 40 to 60 dangles.

2 Wrap the chain around your waist or hips to figure out the length, and add 8–10 in. (20–25cm) for an extender. (My belt is 43 in./1.1m.) Three or four links (about 1 in./2.5cm) from one end of the chain, attach a dangle to a link. Complete the wraps.

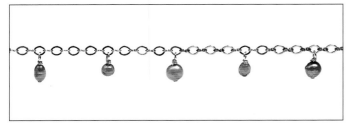

3 Attach another dangle to the chain, three or four links from the previous dangle. Make sure to attach each dangle to the same side of the chain. Continue attaching dangles every three or four links until the beaded part fits around your waist or hips.

4 Attach seven or eight more dangles to make an extender. Check the fit, and add or remove dangles if you need to. Trim the chain after the last dangle. Open a jump ring (Basics). Attach a lobster claw clasp to the other chain end, and close the jump ring.

supplies

- **40–60** 4–8mm beads, in five styles
- 3½–5 ft. (1.1–1.5m) chain, 3–7mm links (base metal chain from Chelsea's Beads)
- **40–60** 1½-in. (3.8cm) head pins
- 3–4mm jump ring
- lobster claw clasp
- chainnose pliers
- roundnose pliers
- diagonal wire cutters

tip *Use a chain with long and short links rather than a cable chain. It's easier to count the links. Also, make sure a lobster claw clasp can fit through the links.*

Share the fun

A couple of weeks before the party, order a few pounds of junk jewelry. Give each guest a grab bag of stuff to make charm bracelets (p. 59) and mismatched charm earrings (p. 75).

Host a cool jewels party

Now that you can make loops and crimp like a pro, why not share what you've learned with your friends by hosting a jewelry party?

Before the party, put together a kit with supplies for each guest. Include a heavy paper plate with compartments so guests can lay out their designs without beads rolling away. Also, if the jewelry requires plain or wrapped loops, give everyone some practice wire from the craft store or hardware store. If you invited lots of friends, you may want to buy an extra set of inexpensive tools.

Create your own signature designs, or try one of these:

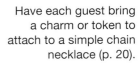

Have each guest bring a charm or token to attach to a simple chain necklace (p. 20).

Buy gemstone strands and pendants to make necklaces (p. 18) and bracelets (p. 44). If you order online, you may get a discounted price for buying a few of the same strands.

Buy alphabet beads and string word bracelets (p. 48). Put letters in bowls so they're easy to reach. Have each person make one for another guest.

During the holidays, whip up a batch of snowflake ornaments (p. 88). If you're feeling the yuletide spirit, donate them to a local hospital or nursing home.

For a quick project, rings (p. 86 and 87) are easy and a good way to use up leftover beads. Buy a bunch of ring findings, head pins, and jump rings. Set out beads and charms and let guests choose their own.

Help your guests with plain and wrapped loops, opening and closing jump rings, and crimping. Once they see you do the basics, they'll know how easy it is to make their own cool jewels.

Where to shop

To buy the basics, try your local bead or craft store. You can ask questions, get a second opinion on your designs, or even take a class. I also like to shop online. Many suppliers offer a print catalog, free shipping, or frequent shopper discounts, so check out these sites:

Artbeads.com artbeads.com

Art Gems artgemsinc.com

Auntie's Beads auntiesbeads.com

Beadalon beadalon.com

The Bead Shop beadshop.com

The Beadin' Path beadinpath.com

Beadissimo beadissimo.com

Bead Needs, LLC beadneedsllc.com

Beads and Pieces beadsandpieces.com

BeadStyle magazine beadstylemag.com

Blue Mud bluemud.com

Charm Factory charmfactory.com

Chelsea's Beads chelseasbeads.com

Da Beads dabeads.com

Earth Echoes earthechoes.biz

eBay ebay.com

Eclectica eclecticabeads.com

Family Glass familyglass.com

Fire Mountain Gems firemountaingems.com

Fusion Beads fusionbeads.com

Goodwill Industries shopgoodwill.com

House of Gems houseofgems.com

JewelrySupply.com jewelrysupply.com

Jo-Ann Stores, Inc. joann.com

Knot Just Beads knotjustbeads.com

Land of Odds landofodds.com

Lima Beads limabeads.com

Lisa Kan Designs lisakan.com

Michaels michaels.com

Olive Glass oliveglass.com

Ornamentea ornamentea.com

Pearlwear pearlwear.com

Planet Bead planetbead.com

Rings & Things rings-things.com

Rio Grande riogrande.com

Ritual Adornments ritualadornments.com

Rupa B. Designs rupab.com

Saki Silver sakisilver.com

Shipwreck Beads shipwreckbeads.com

Soft Flex Company softflexcompany.com

Swarovski create-your-style.com

TLS Designs stores.ebay.com/tls-designs

Urban Maille urbanmaille.com

Vintaj vintaj.com

COOL
jewels

BEADING
PROJECTS
FOR TEENS